# Local Knowledge

*Poems*

B. H. Fairchild

W. W. NORTON & COMPANY

NEW YORK   LONDON

For information about permission to reproduce selections from this book, write
to Permissions, W. W. Norton & Company, Inc., 500 Fifth Avenue, New York,
NY 10110

Manufacturing by Courier Westford
Book design by Lovedog Studio
Production manager: Anna Oler

Library of Congress Cataloging-in-Publication Data
Fairchild, B. H.
Local knowledge : poems / B. H. Fairchild
p. cm.
**ISBN 0-393-32221-1 (pbk.)**
I. Title.
PS3556.A3625L63 2005
811'.54—dc22                                     2005025983

W. W. Norton & Company, Inc.
500 Fifth Avenue, New York, N.Y. 10110
www.wwnorton.com

W. W. Norton & Company Ltd.
Castle House, 75/76 Wells Street, London W1T 3QT

1 2 3 4 5 6 7 8 9 0

*for Patricia Lea Fairchild*

# Contents

# Preface

I wish to thank Jill Bialosky and W. W. Norton for bringing out this new edition of *Local Knowledge*, my second full-length book of poems, which was originally published in 1991 by the *Quarterly Review of Literature* in a single volume that included books by four other poets: Bruce Bond, Judith Kroll, Geraldine C. Little, and Jean Nordhaus. In the years since then, I have often thought of small revisions I would like to have made to some of the poems, and so in this new edition there are minor changes, most simply involving word choice, though I have also rather severely altered the sequence of the poems (originally divided into four parts) and the structure of the title poem.

One of the longest-running and most prestigious small magazines in the history of American poetry, *QRL* ceased publication in 2003 with the death of the poet Ted Weiss, who along with his wife, Renée Weiss, had edited it continuously since its inception in 1943.

I can recall vividly my excitement in reading the hand-written acceptance letter from Ted, and I will always feel grateful for being published in the same series of four or five books to a volume, begun in 1978, that had included the first or second books of such now highly regarded poets as Joan Aleshire, Christopher Bursk, Anne Carson, Reginald Gibbons, Jane Hirshfield, David Keller, Larry Kramer, Reg Saner, and Brian Swann. The first American translation of Wisława Szymborska's *Selected Poems* appeared in this series, as well as *Works and Days* by the brilliant but little-known David Schubert, along with Renée Weiss's beautifully orchestrated "multi-auto-biography" of Schubert.

The manuscripts, letters, and other documents relevant to the long career of *QRL* are now archived at Princeton University and cry out for some enterprising young scholar to write the history of a small magazine that became in effect a relief map of American poetry's journey through the second half of the twentieth century and that also during that period played a major part in the "internationalizing" of American poetry by introducing many younger poets to the work of Hölderlin, Leopardi, Valéry, and Montale in special issues that included translations as well as criticism. I believe it is fair to say that *QRL* published virtually every important American poet of the period (from the later work of the great high moderns to the present, including the early work of Merrill, Hecht, Dickey, James Wright, Merwin, and many others) as well as major contemporary international voices, and even a very meager sampling of the *QRL 50th Anniversary Anthology* would include names such as Amichai, Cavafy, Celan, Char, Mandelstam, Saint John Perse,

Ponge, Seferis. *QRL* also had an involved ongoing relationship with contributors William Carlos Williams and Wallace Stevens, and the correspondence there alone would seem enough to attract high scholarly interest.

Just as I now want to express my appreciation to *QRL* for originally bringing out *Local Knowledge,* so almost fifteen years ago did I travel to Princeton to say this to Ted and Renée in person. They were gracious hosts, showing me around the campus and taking me to lunch at the faculty dining room in the former home of Woodrow Wilson and then afterward to the *QRL* offices. To a Kansas boy who grew up on the stories of F. Scott Fitzgerald, any Ivy League campus is exotic in and of itself, but to stand there where American poetry had been happening for half a century and to look down on the lecture halls and playing fields of *This Side of Paradise* was, well, pretty close to my idea of paradise. And I thank Renée and Ted for that, too.

# Acknowledgments

I wish to thank the National Endowment for the Arts for a fellowship that supported the writing of this book, and the following publications for poems that originally appeared in them (although, in some cases, in different form).

*The American Writer:* "The Woman at the Laundromat Crying 'Mercy'"

*Art/Life:* "December, 1986"

*Black Warrior Review:* "The City of God"

*Cincinnati Review:* "The Robinson Hotel"

*Colorado Review:* "In Another Life I Encounter My Father"

*Georgia Review:* "There Is Constant Movement in My Head"

*Hudson Review:* "The Structures of Everyday Life"

*Jacaranda Review:* "Kansas"

*Oxford Magazine:* "West Texas"

*Prairie Schooner:* "In Czechoslovakia," "Maize," "The March of the
Suicides"

*Puerto del Sol:* "The Soliloquy of the Appliance Repairman"

*RE: Artes Liberales:* "The Doppler Effect," "Strength"

*Salmagundi:* "Language, Nonsense, Desire"

*Southern Poetry Review:* "The Drunk Foreman," "Local
Knowledge," "The Messengers"

*Southern Review:* "In a Cafe near Tuba City, Arizona, Beating
My Head against a Cigarette Machine," "The Last Days,"
"My Mother's Dreams," "Speaking the Names"

*TriQuarterly:* "The Machinist, Teaching His Daughter to Play the
Piano," "Work"


Several of the poems appeared in the chapbooks *The System of
Which the Body Is One Part* (State Street Press) and *Flight* (Devil's
Millhopper Press).

# Local Knowledge

*The local is not a place but a place in a given man—what part of it he has been compelled or else brought by love to give witness to in his own mind. And that is THE form, that is, the whole thing, as whole as it can get.*

—Robert Creeley

# In Czechoslovakia

It is 1968, and you are watching a movie
called *The Shop on Main Street,* about a man—
an ordinary man, a carpenter—in Czechoslovakia,
who is appointed Aryan Controller of a poor button shop
belonging to the widow Lautman, who is old
and deaf and has the eyes of a feverish child.
She smiles in luminous gratitude for almost anything—
the empty button boxes, a photo of her lost daughters,
the man, Tono, who she believes has come to help her.

At the point where the two meet—she, kind but confused,
he, awkward and somewhat ashamed—you notice a woman
in the front row who keeps bending toward the seat
beside her and whispering and letting her hand drift
lovingly toward whomever—a child, you suppose—is there.
The woman's frizzy hair catches the reflected light
from the screen, a nimbus of fire around her head
as she turns to share her popcorn with the child whose
fine blonde hair and green eyes you have begun to imagine.

In the movie Tono has failed to explain his position
to the widow and is acting as her helper in exchange

for monthly payments from the Jewish community.
He is contented, his ambitious wife is enjoying
dreams of prosperity and a heightened sexuality,
it is that terrible time when everyone is happier
than they should be, and then of course the trucks
move in, the dependable gray trucks that have made
life somewhat impossible in the twentieth century.

Now the woman in the front row has returned
to her seat and is handing a Coke to the child
hidden by the chair back, then reaching over
with a handkerchief to wipe the child's mouth
and smile and whisper out of that explosion of hair
she wears. The widow Lautman cannot understand
the trucks or Tono's dilemma that either she must go
or he will be arrested as a collaborator, and as he
stands there pleading, going crazy in her husband's suit

which she has given to him, her eyes widen
like opened fists and she knows now and begins
to shout, *pogrom, pogrom,* with her hands trembling
like moths around her face, and when he panics
and hurls her into the closet to hide her, she falls
and oh Jesus he has killed her and he cries out,
*I am a zero,* but you think, no, no, it's worse,
*you're a man,* and now the woman in the front row
is shouting at the child, it's misbehaved in some way,

and when you look up my God Tono has hung himself
in the suit that belonged to the widow's husband,
the suit he was married in, and then, miraculously,
Tono and the widow are floating arm in arm,
smiling, dancing out into the sun-drenched boulevard,
dancing away from you and history, resurrected
into the world as it might be but somehow cannot be,
a grove of light where the cobbled streets and trees
with their wire skirts are glossy after a soft rain

and the world deepens without darkening and the faces
of everyone are a kind of ovation, and then it's over,
you think, the house lights go up, and you're sitting there
stunned and the woman from the front row walks out
into the aisle with her hand out behind her as if gripping
another, smaller hand. And you see it, though
you don't want to, because you are a man or a woman,
you see that there is nothing there, no child,
nothing, and the woman stops and bends down to speak

to the child that isn't there and she has this smile
of adoration, this lacemaker's gaze of contentment,
*she is perfectly happy,* and she walks on out
into the street where people are walking up and down
and where you will have to walk up and down
as if you were on a boulevard in Czechoslovakia

watching that endless cortege of gray trucks
rumble by in splendid alignment as you go on thinking
and breathing as usual, wreathed in your own human skin.

# In a Cafe near Tuba City, Arizona, Beating My Head against a Cigarette Machine

*. . . the sea shall give up her dead; and the corruptible bodies*
*of those who sleep in him shall be changed, and made like unto*
*his glorious body.*

— The Book of Common Prayer

The ruptured Pontiac, comatose and tilted on three wheels,
seems to sink slowly like a drunken ship into the asphalt.
My wife wanders aimlessly farther into despair and an absence
of traffic, waving invisible semaphores along the embankment.
The infant we have misnamed after a suicidal poet writhes
in harness across my back, her warm urine funneling between
my buttocks, and her yowls rip like sharks through the gray heat.
But still beyond the screams I hear somehow the flutter
of chicken wings, buckets rattling, the howl of spaniels,
and my grandfather's curse grinding against the dull, unjust sky
of God and Oklahoma. I have given the waitress all my money,
and she has taken it, stuffed it into the heart-shaped pocket
    monogrammed
with her ridiculous name, and removed herself to the storeroom
with the cook who wants only to doze through the afternoon lull
undisturbed by a man who has yanked the PALL MALL knob
from the cigarette machine and now beats his head against
the coin return button while mumbling the prayer for the Burial

of the Dead at Sea which his grandmother taught him as a charm
against drowning in the long silences before tornadoes
and floods when Black Bear Creek rose on the Otoe
and the windmill began to shriek like a gang of vampires.
In the shards of the machine's mirror I see the black line
of blood dividing my forehead and a dozen versions of my wife
sobbing now at the screen door while behind her our laundry
has flown free of the Pontiac's wired trunk lid and drifts
like gulls across the vast sea, the difficult sea surrounding
Tuba City, Arizona, and my grandparents walk slowly
toward us over the water in the serene and noble attitude of gods.

# Language, Nonsense, Desire

Professor Ramirez dozes behind the projector,
*Conversación Español* lapping over the bored
shoulders of sophomores who dissolve in the film's
languor of talk and coffee at a sidewalk cafe
in Madrid or Barcelona or some other luminous
Mediterranean dream. The tanned faces rounding
into the Spanish air like bowls of still-life fruit
offer little dialogues about streetcars or feathers
over a clutter of plates and delicate white cups
of mocha blend. The hands of the speakers
are bright birds that lift and tremble among
the anomalies of ordinary life: *piñatas,* cousins
who live in Peru, the last train to Zaragoza.
The speakers are three friends forever entangled
in the syntax of Spanish 101, fated to shape
loose chatter into harmonies of discourse, arias
of locus, *¿Dónde está la casa?* and possession,
*Yo tengo un perro:* Raoul, his dark, hungry
profile immaculately defined against the pallor
of a white beach; the housewife Esmeralda erotic
in her onyx curls, recalling a Catholic childhood,
that same black extravagance pressed against

her pillow as she listened to the nun read stories
and imagined herself as a gaucho, drunk and love-
crazed in the hills of Argentina; and wan Julio,
articulate, epicene, fluttering his pianist's fingers
as he croons melodiously about the rush of time:
*¿Qué hora es? ¿Son las dos? ¡Ay!* And always
in the background along the periphery of syllable
and gesture, the silent pilgrimage of traffic
and commerce and light-dazzled crowds with some
destination, some far blue promise to carry them
through the day, some end to speech and love.

# There Is Constant Movement in My Head

*The choreographer from Nebraska*
*is listening to her mother's cane*
*hammering the dance floor, down, down,*
*like some gaunt, rapacious bird*
*digging at a rotted limb. The mother*
*still beats time in her daughter's head.*

There is constant movement in my head,
the choreographer begins. In Nebraska
I learned dance and guilt from my mother,
held my hands out straight until the cane
beat my palms blue. I was a wild bird
crashing into walls, calming down

only to dance. When Tallchief came down
from New York, a dream flew into my head:
to be six feet tall, to dance the *Firebird*
all in black and red, to shock Nebraska
with my naked, crazy leaps until the cane
shook in the furious hand of my mother.

Well, that day never came. My mother
thought I could be whittled down,
an oak stump to carve into some cane
she could lean on. But in my head
were the sandhill cranes that crossed Nebraska
each fall: sluggish, great-winged birds

lumbering from our pond, the air bird-
heavy with cries and thrumming. My mother
knew. She said I would leave Nebraska,
that small-town life could only pull me down.
Then her hands flew up around her head
and she hacked at the air with her cane.

There are movements I can't forget: the cane
banging the floor, dancers like huge birds
struggling into flight, and overhead,
the choreography of silver cranes my mother
always watched when the wind blew down
from the sandhills and leaves fell on Nebraska.

This dance is the cane of my mother.
The dancers are birds that will never come down.
They were all in my head when I left Nebraska.

# Maize

After Roland Stills fell from the top of the GANO
grain elevator, we felt obliged in some confused,
floundering way as if his hand had just pulled
the red flag from our pockets and we had turned
to find not him but rows of Kansas maize
reeling into the sun, we felt driven to recall
more than perhaps, drunk, we saw: trees squatting
below like pond frogs, mare's tails sweeping the hills,
and the moon in its floppy dress riding low behind
the shock of his yellow hair as, falling, he seemed
to drop to his knees, drunk, passing out, *oh shit,*
with the same stupid grin as when he might recite
Baudelaire in the company of a girl and a small glass
of Cointreau, *Je suis comme le roi d'un pays pluvieux.*
And beyond his eyes blooming suddenly into white
flowers were the lights of houses where our parents
spoke of harvest like a huge wall they would climb
to come again to a new life. Driving along dirt roads
in our trucks, we would look through the scrim of dust
at the throbbing land and rows of red maize whipping past
before the hard heat of summer when the combines
came pushing their shadows and shouldering each other

dark as clouds erasing the horizon, coming down
on the fields to cut the maize, to cut it down
in a country without rain or the grace of kings.

# Child and Dwarf

*ah, but my heart, my bent-over blood,*
*all the distortions that hurt me inside*

—Rilke, "The Dwarf's Song"

Knees under chin beneath a turmoil
of Rodin's struggling torsos, a child sits
watching a woman smaller than a child

striding through the museum foyer.
The tall bronze doors sigh shut.
The woman pauses, then begins circling

the Rodin, stricken by a cylinder
of light breaking through the atrium.
The child's eyes pursue the woman

like a lover's, and a thin smile
curls to lift and draw her slowly
through the widening pool of light.

Now the gnarled fingers of a figure's
outstretched hand hold them there,
blonde hair twisting down their spines,

arms almost touching, girl and woman
watching three men wrestling, it seems,
to escape the prison of their skins.

Dwarf and child turn, then, to see,
eye to eye, the child that isn't,
the child that is, the distortions

of the body, mind, and eye, and
with the shifting light, the sculpture
seems to move beneath a mass of shadows,

the too large heads stretching the tendons
of the neck, the long arms lengthening,
the great hands grasping in the coiling air.

# In Another Life I Encounter My Father

There we are in the same outfield,
a minor league team named after some small
but ferocious animal—the Badgers, say,
or Bulldogs. The town is heavily industrial,
Peoria maybe, and the slap of the fungo bat
keeps us moving over the worn grass—in,
then back, where a blonde drinking a beer
is painted crudely on a white fence.
Big drops of condensation drape the bottle,
which is angled toward her open mouth.
We want to joke about this, but don't.
He is new on the team, and we are uneasy
with each other. When a high one drifts
far to his right, he takes it on a dead run.
He is more graceful than I am, and faster.

In the dugout he offers me a chew,
and we begin to talk—hometown, college ball,
stuff like that. A copy of Rimbaud
sticks out of my pocket, and I give him
the line about *begging the day for mercy.*
He frowns, spitting, working his glove.

We begin to talk politics, baseball
as ideology, more embracing than Marxism.
He seems interested, but something is wrong.
The sky is getting a yellow tinge.
The heavy air droops over my shoulders,
and the locusts begin their harangue.
When I go to the plate, the ball
floats by fat as a cantaloupe, and I
slam it through the left field lights.

I can do no wrong, but we are losing.
The coach, an alcoholic, is beginning
to cry over his second wife. His wails
unnerve us. The catcher is stoned,
and we may have to forfeit. The new guy
is unperturbed and praises me lavishly
on my fine play. In the outfield I point out
Draco and Cassiopeia, almost missing one
that drives me into the fence. I hold
the ball high and tip my cap, the crowd
roars, blood runs down my back. Walking in,
he knows I am playing over my head, but says
nothing. We hear the batboy's shriek,
the coach's tired moan. The locusts
are shredding the air like band saws,
the scoreboard is blazing at the edges,
and we know that the game will never end.

# The Woman at the Laundromat
# Crying "Mercy"

And the glass eyes of dryers whirl
on either side, the roar just loud enough
to still the talk of women. Nothing
is said easily here. Below the screams
of two kids skateboarding in the aisles
thuds and rumbles smother everything,
even the woman crying *mercy, mercy.*

Torn slips of paper on a board swear
Jesus is the Lord, nude photo sessions
can help girls who want to learn, the price
for Sunshine Day School is affordable,
astrology can change your life, any
life. Long white rows of washers lead
straight as highways to a change machine

that turns dollars into dimes to keep
the dryers running. When they stop,
the women lift the dry things out and hold
the sheets between them, pressing corners

warm as babies to their breasts. In back,
the change machine has jammed and a woman
beats it with her fists, crying *mercy, mercy.*

# The Machinist, Teaching His Daughter to Play the Piano

The brown wrist and hand with its raw knuckles and blue nails
      packed with dirt and oil, pause in midair,
the fingers arched delicately,

and she mimics him, hand held just so, the wrist loose,
      then swooping down to the wrong chord.
She lifts her hand and tries again.

*Drill collars rumble, hammering the nubbin-posts.*
      *The helper lifts one, turning it slowly,*
*then lugs it into the lathe's chuck.*

*The bit sheers the dull iron into new metal, falling*
      *into the steady chant of lathe work,*
*and the machinist lights a cigarette, holding*

*in his upturned palms the polonaise he learned at ten,*
      *then later the easiest waltzes,*
*études, impossible counterpoint*

like the voice of his daughter he overhears one night
    standing in the backyard. She is speaking
to herself but not herself, as in prayer,

the listener is some version of herself
    and the names are pronounced carefully,
self-consciously: Chopin, Mozart,

Scarlatti . . . these gestures of voice, and hands
    suspended over the keyboard
that move like the lathe in its turning

toward music, the wind dragging the hoist chain, the ring
    of iron on iron in the holding rack.
His daughter speaks to him one night,

but not to him, rather someone created between them,
    a listener, there and not there,
a master of lathes, a student of music.

# The March of the Suicides

Wherever they move,
the earth crumbles beneath them
and the glass wings of cicadas are raised against the stars.

Like women washing on riverbanks,
some of them kneel and press their palms into the ground,
the lustrations of those who have abandoned the earth.

Pinned on their garments are notes
like those found on school children
whose mothers frown and bend down to read their chests.

Their cries at sunrise are not frightening.
Infants wake to see them swooning into their own shadows,
the bronze shadows over ponds in winter.

Their hands are blue
and their dusty eyes revolve constantly
like moons unmoored from ocean, tree, and stone.

Memory accompanies them everywhere,
an ill-fitting cloak
that makes their shoulders seem luminescent and heavy.

Often, passing beneath mulberry trees
or window ledges, they croon a one-note song,
the sound of a steel ball spinning, perfectly honed.

They will call you only once,
as you sit there in the half-light
and cannot see the ends of your arms.

# The Doppler Effect

When I would go into bars in those days
the hard round faces would turn
to speak something like loneliness
but deeper, the rain spilling into gutters
or the sound of a car pulling away
in a moment of sleeplessness just before dawn,
the Doppler effect, I would have said shrewdly then,
of faces diminishing slightly into the distance
even as they spoke. Their children
were doing well, somewhere, and their wives
were somewhere, too, and we were here
with those bright euphoric flowers
unfolding slowly in our eyes
and the sun which we had not seen for days
nuzzling our fingertips and licking
our elbows. Oh, it was all there,
and there again the same, our heads nodding,
hands resting lightly upon the mahogany sheen
of the bar. Then one of us would leave
and the door would turn to a yellow square
so sudden and full of fire
that our eyes would daze and we would

stare into the long mirrors for hours
and speak shrewdly of that pulling away,
that going toward something.

# The Robinson Hotel

The windows frame a sun in white squares.
    Across the street
the Bluebird Café leans into shadow and the cook
    stands in the doorway.
Men from harvest crews step from the Robinson
    in clean white shirts
and new jeans. They stroll beneath the awning,
    smoking Camels,
considering the crude tattoos beneath their sleeves,
    Friday nights
in San Diego years ago, a woman, pink neon lights
    rippling in rainwater.
Tonight, chicken-fried steak and coffee alone
    at the Bluebird,
a double feature at the PLAZA: *Country Girl*,
    *The Bridges at Toko-Ri.*
The town's night-soul, a marquee flashing orange
    bulbs, stuns the windows
of the Robinson. The men will leave as heroes
    undiscovered.
Their deaths will be significant and beautiful
    as bright aircraft,

sun glancing on silver wings, twisting, settling
　　　into green seas.
In their rooms at night, they see Grace Kelly
　　　bending at their bedsides.
They pass their hands slowly across their chests
　　　and raise their knees
against the sheets. The PLAZA's orange light
　　　fills the curtains.
Cardboard suitcases lie open, white shirts folded
　　　like pressed flowers.

# Toban's Precision Machine Shop

It has just rained, a slow movement of Mahler
drifts from Toban's office in back, the windows
blurred by runnels of grease and dirt, and I walk
into the grease-and-water smell like a child
entering his grandfather's closet. It is a shop
so old the lathes are driven by leather belts
descending like some spiritual harness
from a long shaft beneath the tin roof's peak.

Such emptiness. Such a large and palpable
sculpture of disuse: lathes leaning against
their leather straps, grinding wheels motionless
above mounds of iron filings. Tools lie lead-
heavy along the backs of steel workbenches,
burnished where the morning light leaks through
and lifts them up. Calipers and honing cloths
hang suspended in someone's dream of perfection.

There are times when the sun lingers over
the green plastic panels on the roof, and light
seems to rise from the floor, seems to lift lathes
and floor at once, and something announces itself:

not beauty, but rather its possibility,
and you almost reach out, almost lean forward
to lie down in that wash of bronze light, as if
it would bear you up, would hold you in sleep.

Toban no longer sees the shop advancing
into its day's purchase of light and dark.
He sits in his office among his books
with music settling down on his shoulders
like a warm shawl. He replaces the Mahler
with Schubert, the B-flat sonata, and sends it
unravelling toward me, turning the sound
far above the cluttered silence of the lathes.

# Strength

When with one hand Joseph Little Bear lifted
the drill collar from his foot
and sighed as if waking from a long sleep,
it is odd how we were weakened by this,
how we all became children watching
our fathers wrestling with our uncles
or hoisting a huge cottonwood log on one shoulder
and smiling down to remind us that we did not yet belong
to the world, that strength lay in the lifting
of things heavier and larger than ourselves.

And thus did we return to the washroom
that day with our black hands and pale shoulders
and turned away from the photographs
of bronze women we knew we could never have.
Later that weekend when we carried Little Bear
again from the tavern holding his blood-caked fists
to his chest like crushed roses
and mumbling the prayers and curses
of another language, then too we felt uneasy,

and on the road to his tar-paper shack
something cold fell around us
as we watched the distant fires
of the moon through the branches that passed by overhead.
Little Bear's horse stood waiting in the makeshift corral,
and its head turned so that the one moon-
lit eye came at us like a train in a tunnel of light,
came rushing toward us, beyond strength
or weakness, and Little Bear was singing
and our bodies turned to water and ran slowly out of our lives.

# Speaking the Names

When frost first enters the air
in the country of moon and stars,
the world has glass edges, and the hard glint
of crystals seeping over iron
makes even the abandoned tractor seem all night sky and starlight.

On the backporch taking deep breaths like some miracle cure,
*breathe, let the spirit move you,*
here I am after the long line of cigarettes
that follows grief like a curse, trying to breathe, revive,
in this land of revivals and lost farms . . .

It is no good to grow up hating the rich.
In spring I would lie down among pale anemone and primrose
and listen to the river's darkening hymn, and soon
the clouds were unravelling like the frayed sleeves of field hands,
and ideology had flown with the sparrows.

The cottonwood that sheltered the henhouse is a stump now,
and the hackberries on the north were leveled years ago.
Bluestem hides the cellar, with its sweet gloom of clay walls and
    bottles.

The silo looms over the barn, whose huge door swallowed
     daylight,
where a child could enter his own death.

What became of the boy with nine fingers?
The midwife from Yellow Horse who raised geese?
They turned their backs on the hard life,
and from the tree line along the river they seem to rise now,
her plain dress bronze in moonlight, his wheatshock hair in
     flames.

Behind me is a house without people. And so, for my sake
I bring them back, watching the quick cloud of vapor that
     blooms
and vanishes with each syllable: *O. T.* and *Nellie Swearingen,*
their children, *Locie, Dorrel, Deanie, Bill,*
and the late *Vinna Adams,* whose name I speak into the bright
     and final air.

# The Last Days

Out here, where the high wires pitch and whine
and bluestem rakes the tops of my wrists,
the sky seems to worry itself into dusk,
clouds thinning into mare's tails,
a rasp of grackles keening into the west wind,
tumbleweeds that lunge, then hang
on the rusted barbs of hard, angry possession.

Rows of stubble veer toward the poplar trees
that shield my house from blowing topsoil,
and through the branches a lighted window shines:
my son and daughter lost in books,
my wife awash with the colors of the TV screen.
And the pane of glass that comes between us
seems as distant, as final, as the stars.

For hours I have walked the fences
of these separate fields where the dying light
grows long and mottled over bunches
of shorn maize stalks and rotted fenceposts,
where last night's dream comes flashing back
like the sputtering red lights of the town's
last elevator warning off low flights:

My grandmother holds my face between her palms
and pleads, *release the dead, let them rise up*
*and walk the bankrupt fields and turn them*
*back to wilderness, the way we found them.*
*Let those who died to hold the land be gathered*
*in the failing town, then let the sun reclaim*
*the earth, let it burn, oh, let it all come down.*

# Fire and Water

Old girl. She mumbled like an idle child,
clapping, endlessly babbling, *the fire,*
*the house,* ankle-deep in slush, junk
bludgeoned with smoke, blasted by fire-hoses.
*Oh, if things could only die,* she sobbed,
collecting the wounded: porcelain angel
statuettes blackened with ash now;
charred clumps of photos; the WWII
souvenir silk pillow, a smoke-gray wad
jammed beneath the still steaming couch.
*Things,* marginalia of a house, a life
between walls hung with handwork, knitted
shawls and quilts where now what was left of
wallpaper drooped blistered and fringed
in brown scallops.
                   Fire and water:
flames sluicing over windowsills, bleeding
around corners lurid as snakeweed
from the trampled side yard; afterward,
black pools of ooze, thick soup of memory,
a wrecked lamp stranded like a crane
in a drained lake. Each day I trundled

sludge and garbage from the drowned house,
and each night she rose from the one
untouched bed and slipped into the alley,
lifted piles of rubble under the ragged
shawl of starlight, then lugged them in
and stumbled back for more. One night
she banged a ruined hatrack through
the gutted kitchen, and I woke
to bellow in her dumb ears, *It's trash,*
*shit, leave it!* Truckloads kept
coming back, kept haunting my burnt-out
mornings until I gave up.
                              I stocked
the new apartment with kitchen ware,
copper pans and big moon-bright skillets.
The white tile floor shone like glazed ice,
the yellow wall paint still too wet
to touch. We stood together at the sink
washing our hands and peering down
at the pool raging in the flames of noon
and cries of swimmers bruising the air.
How young they were! and how beautiful,
with their keen, anonymous faces and
their hands raised, as if pushing something
back, and their lean bodies just lightly
scorched by the diminishing fire of the sun.

# The Messengers

At twilight baseball fields make their green cries
of abandonment, the dust lying still on the base paths,
the outfield thick with the secrets of mushrooms.

On Crosstown 30 Louise Johnson is hauling
baseball trophies in her pickup.
They gleam like the backs of dolphins
or rows of votive candles flickering in the half-light.
They are Brahmin, the red dot of the sun is on their foreheads.

Louise points her cigar toward the horizon,
the little bronze men press on, shoulder to shoulder.
They plunge through the failed landscape—
the housing tracts, the smog's death-shroud, the stolen water
of the Los Angeles aqueduct:
                                    *Receive us,*
*let us be among the earth's children*
*who await the withheld promise, the floating fast ball,*
*the fat knuckler that turns like a distant planet.*

The entire Little League is mad with desire.
Floodlights shatter the darkness,

the shouts of lost fathers litter the diamond.
In the monastic silences of right field, thin arms
and a glove wide as the moon are raised against the ball's long arc.

Here comes Louise, pickup clattering
like an exhausted army, her left arm lifted
toward the indifferent sky. Cities lie swollen
with lights along the valley. Statuettes are waiting
to be born. Inside us, children are praying.

# Local Knowledge

*It seems hard to find an acceptable answer to the question*
*of how or why the world conceives a desire, and discovers*
*an ability, to see itself, and appears to suffer the process.*
*That it does so is sometimes called the original mystery.*
>                      —G. Spencer Brown, *Laws of Form*

### I.

A rusted-out Ford Fairlane with red star hubcaps
skids up to Neiderland Rig Local No. 1
heaving Travis Deeds into a swirl of dust
and rainbowed pools of oil and yellow mud.

Rows of drill collars stand in racks and howl
in the blunt wind. Chain and hoist cable
bang the side of a tin bunkhouse as men stunned
with hangovers wake to the drum of a new day.

Crowding around the rig floor where the long
column of iron reaches straight down through rock
and salt water, Travis and the men grab
the big tongs and throw them on, then off,

hauling up one length of pipe, then another
as the bit drags out of the hole, coming up
with crushed rock and shark's teeth from old strata
once under ocean. The drawworks lurches, rumbling

loud enough to smother talk, and the men
work under the iron brand of the noon sun
until mud covers them. Their arms and faces
blacken, and gas fumes sting their eyes.

Two hundred feet up, the crown block pulleys
wail on their axles like high wires, keening.
Travis leans back to see the black mud hose curl
into a question mark looming from earth to sun.


## II.


*Dear Father,*
*            As you can see I have*
*come pretty far north with this bunch*
*almost to Amarillo in a stretch*
*of wheat field flat and blowed out as any*

*to be seen in West Texas. All things*
*are full of weariness, as the man says,*
*and I am one of those things, dog-tired*
*and not fit to shoot. I am very glad*

to hear you are back with your church
in Odessa if that is what you want
and if that old bottle does not bring
you down again though it is a comfort

to me, which you do not want to hear,
but alone up there in the crow's nest
with the wind screaming at me
and that old devil moon staring down

and nothing all around, you get to thinking
you are pretty much nothing yourself.
But I am all OK, staying out
of trouble, and I do not know where

I am going in this world but am looking
as always for a fat paycheck and then
I will be home again. Take good care
of yourself.

Your loving son,
Travis

## III.

Travis Deeds' tongue, throat, wide mouth:
singers of broken tunes and his father's hymns
in dry creek beds alone with Jack Daniel's
and the arc of night, the revolving stars.

The eyes pink from booze, dust, and sunlight,
sleepless beneath a football scar that slices
the left eyebrow like a scythe, readers
of Job and Ecclesiastes, crazed in moonlight.

Belly, back, shoulders pale as eggs,
once-broken arm bent slightly, hands mottled
with scraped knuckles and blue fingernails
that thrum like drumfish with the blood's pulse.

Birthmark like a splash of acid on one thigh,
darkening hair of the loins, sad cock, legs thick
as stumps, knees yellow-brown with old bruises,
ludicrous feet, small toes curled like snails.

Slowly the traveling block lifts his body
to the rig's top. Blond hair blazing, he sings
flat against the hard wind, rising, staring down
into the rig's black strata, the fossil kingdom.

**IV.**

*Dearest son,*

What gain has the worker
from his toil? *I'm a little short here,*
*and if you could spare maybe fifty?*
*Am back on my feet, though, feisty*

*and full of the Word.* So I turned
to consider wisdom and madness
and folly, *and so should you for one*
*of these days God will show His face*

*to you as He has to me, you think*
*your alone in this world, that your*
*nothing, but you are not, believe me.*
*There is more to life than sweat*

*and dirt and oil and fat paychecks.*
*Remember,* better is a handful
of quietness than two hands full
of toil and a striving after wind.

*I know this in my poor banged-up soul.*
*I hope you can come home soon*
*for it is lonely as hell here, that old wolf*
*scratching at my door.*

*Love,*

*Avon*

## V.

Gargantuan plates move over the mantle of the earth.
The jammed crust up-thrusts and rivers spill down,
dumping red dirt in layers, choking themselves dry.
On the west, the Pecos River; on the east,

canyons of the high plains: Palo Duro,
Tule, Casa Blanca, Quitaque, Yellow House.
Calcium bubbles up to form the caprock.
Sod grass spreads under the wind. The dirt holds.

Around the rig now, plowed fields lose the dirt
in gusts, and roughnecks breathe through rags
like small-time bandits. Five miles east, a gray wolf
drags its kill beneath a jagged branch of mesquite.

Under the raucous sky sandhill cranes ruffle
the pond water with their wings, lumbering into flight.
Everywhere the flat land has given up its wheat
and maize, and dust rises along the horizon

like a huge planet out of orbit, colliding.
Travis Deeds, greasing the crown block,
leans against the wind and sees the open mouth
of the sun slowly drowning in the brown air.

## VI.

*Dear Father,*

*Enclosed is a check*
*for fifty bucks, please hang onto it.*
*Good news here. The geologist took*
*what is called a core sample and says*

*that it is a sure thing this time.*
*As for your letter, you say not*
*to feel like nothing, but it seems to me*
*there is alot to be said for nothing.*

*The other night I was alone*
*with just the moon and stars*
*and the locusts buzzing away*
*and could look down the hole*

*into the nothing of the earth*
*and above into the nothing of the sky*
*and there I was in the middle*
*of it all until I was nothing too*

*not even Travis Deeds but just the eye*
*that the world uses to look at itself.*
*So maybe that is a place in the world,*
*not that you would agree. But I am*

*on day shift now and if the geologist*
*is right and we are right next door*
*to pay dirt, I should be home soon*
*with my sack full.*
                              *Your loving son,*
                                       *Travis*


**VII.**


Crew, drawworks, the whole rig floor are dragged
under the dirt storm, roughneck shouts sinking
beneath the wind's harangue, the berserk clatter
of chains, cable, bunkhouse roof yanking loose.

And for a while in the sudden rush and whirl
the body clings to the crown block, grease-slick
hands grasping, then spilling like fish over
the iron rails as the false night swallows

the land the way the land folds its creatures
into bedrock fossils. The body is blown free.
The arms wheel, the legs blunder like tossed sticks,
the soft earth surrounds and pulls him down.

Blood batters the heart in flight, pounding
like the flailing wings of cranes, the quickening

breath of the wolf returning to his kill,
the mesquite branch shaking in the nervous wind.

*Put forth thy hand now and touch his bone and flesh.*
And the men gather where he slams the ground,
where the body is the obedient son of gravity,
where the hands claw the thickening dust, where

the buckled spine rages, where the unknowable God
does not speak the unknowable answer and the great wing
folds and unfolds and once more under the sun's
long pull the wind makes its hollow yowl of lament.

# Kansas

Leaning against my car after changing the oil,
I hold my black hands out and stare into them
as if they were the faces of my children looking
at the winter moon and thinking of the snow
that will erase everything before they wake.

In the garage, my wife comes behind me
and slides her hands beneath my soiled shirt.
Pressing her face between my shoulder blades,
she mumbles something, and soon we are laughing,
wrestling like children among piles of old rags,

towels that unravel endlessly, torn sheets,
work shirts from twenty years ago when I stood
in the door of a machine shop, grease-blackened,
and Kansas lay before me blazing with new snow,
a future of flat land, white skies, and sunlight.

After making love, we lie on the abandoned
mattress and stare at our pale winter bodies
sprawling in the half-light. She touches her belly,
the scar of our last child, and the black
prints of my hands along her hips and thighs.

# Saipan

After the war,
the men, the tired men,
turned inside their bodies, turned
away as the light crumbled
over the park benches where they lay
under newspapers and held bottles
like sleeping babies to their chests.

My father would say, *they never
returned, they never quite came back.*
Everywhere, the arms of men
in rolled brown sleeves, tattoo
like a bruise—SEMPER FI,
*always faithful*—blue heart rippling

as the hand flipped ashes
from a Lucky Strike in the back booth
of a neighborhood bar
or a pool hall where green fields
lay before us like small countries and the arms
moved slowly back and forth behind a gauze of smoke.

At twilight we would see the men in their giant shadows
watering lawns, walking circles within circles
in white undershirts that blazed with the day's last light,
or fishing alone on piers,
the rod delicately held, eyes
reaching across the Pacific to its burnished rim.

I thought they were dead, somehow.
At night resting my head on my father's pillow,
the silk one embroidered with SAIPAN
in flames from a dragon's mouth,
I would think of the dead
and be afraid of their gray eyes and blue arms

and sink into my dreamless sleep
and the long dark fields of nothing.

# December, 1986

Dry socket of the solstice,
dull rub of a turning year.
Neighborhood bars begin to fill.
Overhead, new weather spreads like traffic.

Winter dialectic:
the brewery dispenses men and beer each evening,
drinking day away too soon,
taverns crammed with short lives,
long nights.

I'm in Hermann's,
huddling with friends like thieves.
Voices collect in clouds,
laboring-class lives thick,
intricate as snow settling into mounds
of soft syllables, close and not cold.

# My Mother's Dreams

Huddled with your trembling sisters
under pounds of patchwork quilts the night
Black Bear Creek spilled over the Otoe,
you dreamed green meadows, white fences,
and sloe-eyed, smiling cows that never
needed milking. In Oak City, selling
shoes to Ginger Rogers, you drank nickel
beer after work, elbow to silk elbow
with a good-looking blond later known
as Pretty Boy Floyd. Your dreams hooted
like Depression trains, you said, hobos
leaping into ditches, then springing up
like cartoon bears to croon lullabies
the way the Andrews Sisters sang "Argentine
Nights." And rushing through the tunnel
of the war's long night, the usual Freudian
mob of spiders, floating fish, and falling
teeth must have raised you up to sit, alone,
beneath a single light where you browsed
through photographs of my father, tan
and shirtless, on an island like the island
from the week before. *My own flesh and*

*blood,* you said, when my grandmother died,
and I wondered if you dreamed that way,
violence as metaphor for the ways we live
and die. On V-Day in San Jose you woke
to dirigibles and apricots, Chagall's
green sky. Over oranges and coffee
you told your friend the dream of flowers
within flowers, red petals falling away
to a cobble street where couples strolled
through waves of sunlight and smiled and
smiled again,

              and later, one night after
making love, you dream a dense, slow dream
of caves, paths, streams leading to a road
that winds forever, and there, the white
rabbit behind the dark hedge, there I am,
and in the morning over breakfast, you say
to my father, *I had the strangest dream,*
and you go on in that loose meander
of dream talk, and he almost listens,
humming, feeling the sun's slow touch,
idly stroking the perfect rim of his cup.

# Photograph of a College Football Team, 1927

*Ohi ombre vane, fuor che ne l'aspetto!*

*—Purgatorio*

Before the shutter closes, before the light has gathered,
the one with Nietzsche eyebrows and granite jaw glances
to his right nervously as though drawn to the edge of things,
drifting for the errant long pass, the cruel possibility
that two years of seminary and mental collapse will never reveal.

In the back row the broad face of a Navajo
hovers over the landscape of his shoulders.
The tongue of his own language ripples through him
like an explosion of birds from a thicket.
It is morning, the dawn light lying down in a dream of horses.

On his left a hog-nosed boy grips
the ball hard with blunt fingers, hair parted down the middle
straight as the furrow behind his father's plow in Salina, Kansas.
He is walking away from a white frame house,
a sky half-black with a dust cloud, an absence of trees.

Like auras around their bruised, mortal bodies,
the reflected lights of the flash seem to cloak them
in their unlived lives, the future that looms, diminishing,
the long walk through the coliseum tunnel when the cries
have died away and the rumble of cleats against pavement rolls

through darkness louder and louder. The gargantuan center
must have slumped like a god when he walked away from defeat,
for here he sits brooding, black hair drooping into his eyes,
still listening into the white silence
between the snap and the clatter of shoulderpads.

But the one seated slightly apart on the front row is staring
straight through the camera. His eyes and child's face remind me
of that photograph of Rimbaud where the murderous smirk
is just beginning at the corners of the mouth. The electric hair,
the slender arms and hands, the way the head tilts back just so—

this is the one who knows, and moments before
making that long climb toward sleep, I see him standing quite still
in a green field watching the black hole in the center
of the ball's perfect spiral, the blurred rim of crowd and stadium
and the huge bodies falling, then rising, from the fallen earth.

# The Structures of Everyday Life

In the shop's nave, where the wind bangs sheets
of tin against iron beams, barn sparrows
quarrel like old lovers. At five o'clock
the lathes wind down from their long flight.
Burnt coils of steel loom from collecting bins.

In the washroom photographs of wives and lovers
look down on the backs of men pale as shells.
Brown wrists and black hands lather and shine
in the light of one dim lamp, and blue shirts
hang like the stilled hands of a deaf-mute.

When the foreman sees his raw face in the mirror,
he turns away, shy as a young girl, sick of iron
and rust, the dead sun of the day's end. After
washing, his wet hair gleams in the open door
and he begins his dream of women in cool rooms.

Gusts seep through tin, making the thin music
men live by. Drill pipe they scar knuckles on
clangs restless as planets on the rack outside.
The ten-ton hoist drags its death chain. The sky
is a gray drum, a dull hunger only the plains know.

Like eremites at prayer, the men kneel to lace
their shoes, touching the worn heels of a life.
When they leave, the faces on their locker doors
turn back to darkness. Each man shoulders the sun,
carries it through the fields, the lighted streets.

# Michael Blum Cuts His Brother's Hair

Hair and leaves fall together under the cottonwood,
under the wide eaves behind our mother's house
where Karl, a huge man whose life in iron and steel
has ruined his hands with bruises, sits slumped,
legs crossed, and watches red locks sweep across
the sheet that laps over his knees. He and Mike
are quiet as women folding precious linens
and have not spoken to each other in seven years.

In a gray stubble field where dust devils whipped across
wire fences, our brothers came to blows over
land and money and rightful shares. Then they fell
to silence, two boarded houses standing side by side,
one red truck beside a black at Neiderland's Cafe
on weekday mornings. But from boyhood, Mike, the elder,
did the family barbering, and now we watch the hair
fall and drift across dry leaves and yellow grass.

As the wind picks up and the branches sway and scrape
like blown papers, Mike hums his song, and the words
rise secretly in our minds, *Meine Ruh ist hin, Mein Herz
ist Schwer. . . .* Mother takes up her needlework,

frowning into the long silence, staring at the two
broad faces that mirror her husband, our father,
whose nails held red dirt, hands coarse as rope
against her back, bed creaking as he rose at dawn.

# The Soliloquy of the Appliance Repairman

They bring me their broken toasters,
chrome-dulled and shorted on lumps of grease,
twisted Mixmasters with mangled blades
and bent spindles punch-drunk
and beaten into an early grave.
And I, healer and name-brand magician,
I must raise them from the dead,
prop them up and coax their failed motors
into the life signs of hum and whir.

They go out, they come back,
these wounded, cracked plastic-and-chrome marvels
of the mediocre, of the watery omelette
and bland, confused margarita.
We should learn from our mistakes:
the lawnmower plugged with muddy oil
will foul again, and again
the nightmare ice maker will vomit
its perfectly formed cubes into the void.
Freon again and oh ever again freon
spewing through the endless circuitry of the freezer,
thumping along, hissing through leaks.

The two girls who lugged in
the computerized cappuccino machine,
chattering and letting their bright eyes
and flashing hands erase the shadows
of the shop—how could they have known my limits:
the modern and high-tech, the microwave ovens,
for instance, with their digital readouts
and soft little gongs that puzzled me
almost into retirement months ago.
Give it up, my wife said
*you're as obsolete as they are,*
pointing to the prewar junk piling up unclaimed.

The girls frowned and took it back.
Hunching their shoulders like old women,
they stumbled out, letting the door bang shut,
flinging the shop back into darkness.
I have learned from the inventions of history,
but I live in the age of wonders,
of the self-contained and irreparable,
where I stand and watch
the small, good things of my hands
drifting far away into the corners of my life.

# Sheets

Morning rides its gray horse
over the four-sided gambrel roofs
heavy with new snow,
and I imagine your mother
behind the one lighted window
sewing the hems of sheets, curtains,
clothes for your children,

and thinking of the vacant house
where as children we would spread sheets
over the willow trees in the side yard.
From Mrs. Tate's across the street
they must have looked like giant mushrooms,
a great, slumbering cloth forest
risen suddenly from the hands of children.
And at night, how strange it was,
peeling away a sky of sheets to reveal
another sky with its purple going to black,
its cold air and stars rushing in
through the opened branches.

We would walk home
dragging the sheets over our shoulders,
tired and resigned as our fathers coming home from work,
or Greek actors tossing their masks onto the grass,
already considering the burdens
of family, lovers, money. But again,

the next day there we were,
our arms full of folded sheets,
and we would spread them out carefully
and begin to place them over the willow trees.

# Work

*Work is a transient form of mechanical energy by means
of which certain transformations of other forms of energy
are brought about through the agency of a force acting through
a distance. . . . Work done by lifting a body stores mechanical
potential energy in the system consisting of the body and the
earth. Work done on a body to set it in motion stores mechanical
kinetic energy in the system of which the body is one part.*
— *Handbook of Engineering Fundamentals*

## I. Work

Drill collars lie on racks and howl
in the blunt wind. A winch truck waits
in the shop yard beside an iron block,
hook and cable coiling down, dragging
through dirt that blows in yellow gusts.

East across a field where the slag sky
of morning bends down, a man walks away
from a white frame house and a woman
who shouts and waves from the back porch.
He can hear the shop doors banging open.

Inside, where the gray light lifts dust
in swirls, tools rest like bodies dull
with sleep. The lathe shudders and
starts its dark groan, the chuck's jaw
gripping an iron round, the bit set.

Outside, the man approaches the iron block,
a rotary table, judging its weight,
the jerk and pull on the hoist chain.
A bad sun heaves the shadow of his house
outward. He bends down. A day begins.


## II. The Body

Looping the chain through the block's eyes,
he makes a knot and pulls the cable hook through.
The winch motor starts up, reeling in cable slowly

until it tightens, then drops to a lower gear
and begins to lift. The motor's whine brings
machinists to the shop windows, sends sparrows

fluttering from highwires where the plains wind
gives its bleak moan and sigh. When the brake
is thrown, the block jerks and sways five feet

above the earth, straining to return, popping
a loose cable thread and making the gin poles
screech in their sockets like grief-stricken women.

From the house the man is lost in the blaze of a sun
gorged to bursting and mirrored in the shop's
tin side. The block hangs, black in the red air.


### III. The Body and the Earth

Beneath the rotary table the man reaches up
to remove the huge bearings, and oil winds
like a rope down his arm. He places
each bearing big as a pendulum in the sun

where it shines, swathed in grease.
It is the heart of the day, and he feels
the sudden breeze cool his face and forearms,
wet now with the good sweat of hard work.

The wind scrapes through stubble, making
a papery sound that reminds him of harvest:
him, his father, the field hands crowded around
a beer keg to celebrate the week's cut, dirt

drying to mud on their damp faces, leaving
bruises and black masks. Now, kneeling
in the block's cool shadow, he watches clods
soak up the brown pools of oil and sweat.


### IV. The System of Which the Body Is One Part

On the downside of the workday,
when the wind shifts and heat stuns the ground
like an iron brand, the machinists lean
into the shadow of the shop's eaves
and gulp ice water, watching the yard hand now

as he struggles in his black square
to slip each bearing back in place, each steel ball
that mirrors back his eyes, the stubble field, the shop,
the white frame house, the sun, and everything beyond,
the whole circumference of seen and unseen, the world

stretching away in its one last moment
when the chain makes that odd grunting noise,
and sighs *click,* and then *click,* and sings through the eyes
of the block as it slams the ground and the earth takes
the thud and the men freeze and the woman strolls out to see
what has happened now in the system of which the body is one part.

# Angels

Elliot Ray Neiderland, home from college
one winter, hauling a load of Herefords
from Hogtown to Guymon with a pint of
Ezra Brooks and a copy of Rilke's *Duineser*
*Elegien* on the seat behind him, saw the ass-end
of his semi gliding around in the side mirror
as he hit ice and knew he would never live
to see graduation or the castle at Duino.

In the hospital, head wrapped like a gift
(the nurses stuck a bow on top), he said
four flaming angels crouched on the hood, wings
spread so wide he couldn't see, and then
the world collapsed. We smiled and passed a flask
around. Little Bill and I sang "Your Cheatin'
Heart," and laughed, and then a sudden quiet
put a hard edge on the morning, and we left.

*Siehe, ich lebe,* Look, I'm alive, he said,
leaping down the hospital steps. The nurses
waved, white dresses puffed out like pigeons
in the morning breeze. We roared off in my Dodge,

*Behold, I come like a thief!* he shouted to the town
and gave his life to poetry. He lives, now,
in the south of France. His poems arrive
by mail, and we read them and do not understand.

# Dust Storm

The churning wind thickened to a brown pond,
a clod, grit between my teeth, lungs sucking
clotted air like wings beating on a dirt bank.

It filled the shop, and the windows above
the lathes sank under a ton of dust that coiled
where chinks in the tin roof sent down shafts

of light. The bookkeeper raged and slapped the panes
of his glass cage, his shouts vague as fog.
We could not see our hands in front of our eyes

when the foreman slid the big front door shut
in the dark, the sullen, rank dark that washed
over us as we pressed red rags to our faces.

For hours we lay on the wooden platforms
beside our lathes or stumbled toward
the shop's center and huddled there like thieves

before an open fire, the night-dust sifting
around us until we were old men with gray hair,
and black creases across our foreheads.

When the windows began yellowing
and the floor paled and our hands came floating
back from the pond bottom, the foreman

dragged the huge door slowly open, and this
is what still comes in my dreams: the glacier
of light that moved down from the horizon,

came lunging into the great cave of the shop,
that iron light rumbling toward us,
grinding and shattering the stale air,

a world of light, a sun bludgeoning our eyes,
blinding the town laden with dirt behind us,
and beneath that flaming square, the men

in their little silhouettes, like children pulled
from the smothering earth, the blind, burnt
figures of children who raised their hands

in joy and terror and flashed their eyes
beneath layers of dust, coming into the light
as it moved down and embraced them and took them up.

# The City of God

Everything is as it should be.

Water and light, for instance, have not changed.

The beasts of the field refuse to be beautiful.
They harbor enormous secrets. Their boredom is exquisite.

Grief is migratory. Seasonally it is seen flying
in a new direction in its distinctive V pattern.

The scene of one's childhood is always there
and never revisited: the garage out back, the yellow Studebaker
with mud flaps, the broken water heater, the smell of ammonia.

Someone is always telling a story.

The abandoned shoe on the roadside contains
the memory of Proust. The tin siding banging in the wind
is the Schubert two-cello quintet.

Stars and planets are still stars and planets,
and there is not the remotest chance of ever voyaging to one.

Sleep is optional.

In moments of depression you can go to the back window
and see wild deer crossing the lawn. They freeze,
sensing your presence, and will not move until you do.

Disasters happen every two or three years and everyone survives.

Desire is a dream of blue meadows and chestnut trees.
Fulfillment is the clamor of rain against palm leaves as you dream.

Falling occurs, but without a sinking feeling. Rising occurs,
but without the spiritual implications.

Politicians are kites with heavy tails.
Children have given up on them and tossed them idly by.

Your grandfather's ivory dominoes, long misplaced,
are rediscovered daily.

The old library is just the way it used to be, only more so.

Baseball is played all year.
The Dodgers have returned to Brooklyn.

On summer evenings the shadows move backward
into the branches of trees, leaving behind traces of sound
somewhat like Erik Satie heard from a distance.

Everything is as it was.
Everything is as it will be.

Imperfection is a mark of divinity. God is praised
for his lack of talent.

# West Texas

My red Ford running to rust idles
along the roadside, one headlight
swinging out across the plains,
the other blind. In the rear window
dawn light spills over my children
sprawling tangled in the backseat
beneath an army blanket. My wife
sleeps in front where the radio loses
itself in static, and even Del Rio
is a distant shout. From rig
to rig like this every few months,
the road looming toward more sky,
bunchgrass, sometimes a stooped,
ragged clump of trees. Always
a thin curtain of dust in the air.
Coffee sours through the night,
and I toss the grounds like seeds
from another country over the dry
shoulder. Driving high and sleepless,
I dream awake: faces like strange
gray flowers form and vanish,
my father kneeling in the road, then

looking up. *Stay put, let the land
claim you,* he always said. But here
men own you and the land you drill,
and you move on. My one headlight
dims in the morning light. The other
mirrors back the road, the whitening
sky. Far ahead a hawk is sweeping
into view on wide, black wings.

# The Drunk Foreman

The tossed bottle shatters on a derrick boom,
littering the ironyard. The foreman, shit-faced
with cuts and bruises from a fight, hurls curses
at a moonless sky blank as a bald tire.

Silent, he slumps against the holding rack
to watch the plains in its hard sleep, the way
the earth waits, unwinding the long breath
that outlives men, grinding stone on stone

like the clenched jaw of nightmare. Blown
stubble scrapes gravel in the wind's gust,
and he bangs the hoist chain on pipe, shouting
down every woman who won't have him. Drunk,

he's deaf to the earth's groan and the scream
behind his eyes when he sees his life nailed
flat across the fields the way the yard light
throws down a lone scrub oak's frayed shadow.

One more pint and he's blind, photos of ex-wife
and kids washed pale as bone in his backpocket.
Dumb and bootless, he tumbles into childhood:
dirt farms and thin-wristed women who sang hymns.

Then sleep. His head drops back, skin on steel.
The ground that rolls beneath his dangling hand
reveals a sun still there. The men gather with
coffee, bandages, pleas that sound like prayers.

# L'Attente

The little man sitting at the top of the stairs
looked up at me through eyes dark and unreachable
as stones at the bottom of a pond, and said,
*Waiting is the brother of death.*

In Degas' painting, a woman dressed
in the native costume of death waits
seated on a bench beside her daughter,
a ballerina in blue ribbons and white
crinoline who is bent over slightly
as if she might be ill, ill with waiting,
the harness of the future heavy
around her neck. The mother leans forward,
elbows resting on thighs, and holds
her umbrella out before her in a kind
of resignation, a dropped semaphore,
a broken code. She is beyond language,
and though you cannot see her eyes
beneath the wide brim of her black hat,
something about the jaw and chin, some
thin line of shadow, tells you the eyes
are set in the dazed stare of memory,

the white gloves she wears are the white dresses
of childhood, the white Sunday mornings
narrowing toward the vanishing point
like rows of sycamore along the boulevard.

I said to the little man at the top
of the stairs, *Yes, I know, I am waiting, too.*
And I invited him in for a cup of tea.
Then we sat down at the table on the balcony
drinking our tea, not speaking, warm
in each other's company, like children
waiting for a ballet class to begin,
waiting for the dancing to begin.

# Afterword: Lathework

As a child in West Texas, I am standing beside my father as he works a machine lathe at a shop in one of several dusty oilfield towns, usually boomtowns, that we would move through. As a boy in the small town of Liberal, Kansas, I am standing in front of the old library on the corner of Third Street and Kansas Avenue reading Ernest Thompson Seton's *Biography of a Grizzly*. As a young man I am sitting in a movie theater witnessing the scene of the mother and child described in the poem, "In Czechoslovakia." I will never forget these particular scenes. Standing in a grocery line, running on a quarter-mile track, watching my son play a Little League game, waiting for a stoplight to change, I will find myself turning one of these images over again in my mind and knowing that this is why I write poems.

The first image, I was to discover, holds the model for everything I have written, especially poems: lathework. In machine shops in Houston, Lubbock, Midland, and Snyder, Texas, I would as a boy stand on the wooden ramp next to my father and watch his hands move gracefully and efficiently over the lathe, maneuvering the levers and rotary handles and making the bit move in and out, back and forth, as the huge chuck spun a section of drill pipe in its iron grip. Once he had the bit set just right, having measured the cut with the calipers, he would let go, and a steady spiral of blue steel shaving would coil out into the darkness, dropping with a hiss into the milky mixture of oil and water below. He would then lean back, light a cigarette, pour himself a cup of coffee, and breathe slowly in that easy, contented way of someone sure of his craft, pleased with his own expertise, confident that the thing was going well, that it was going to be a precise, skillful piece of work.

Almost no words would pass between us. There were only the rumble and occasional whine of the lathe, the damp whisper of the shavings, and the surrounding darkness of the immense cathedral of the shop. That, and the mingled odors of oil and water and sweat and khaki, for my father always wore, like a uniform, a starched khaki workshirt and trousers and a pair of Boss Walloper gloves. But there was no talk, no words. I wanted to talk, wanted to trouble him out of the mystery of his pure world of work with a small boy's foolish questions, but the same instinct that kept me quiet in church each Sunday kept me quiet now. There were the machinist and the silence and the constant lesson, repeated with each drill collar, each cut of the bit, of a small thing done well.

Things and words. The words came early and in different ways: whole days spent in bed with bronchitis while words floated disembodied from radio dramas in another room where my mother was ironing, late nights at family reunions when booze had loosened the tongues of my usually silent father and his brothers so that they began to tell the stories about growing up in Oklahoma that I never tired of hearing, afternoons with my father at oil rigs where I would listen to the roughnecks cursing each other in that wonderfully inventive way that seemed to make an art of swearing. But words as a world, a separate reality as pure and hermetically enclosed as the world of lathework, did not open to me until one day on a street corner in Liberal, Kansas. We had just moved there from West Texas, and my parents had gone into the bank across the street to open a checking account, leaving me to amuse myself in the town's tiny storefront library. I browsed around, amazed to learn from the ancient one behind the desk that I was permitted to take books home, as many as four at a time. I checked out *Biography of a Grizzly*, stepped outside, and leaned against the stoplight completely absorbed in the book and oblivious to the swirl of traffic and people around me. I cannot forget the exhilaration I felt at the time, the centripetal pull of the words, the feeling that I was at the center of something, that between myself and the words on the page was a world bearing significance and authenticity, a world that somehow existed not outside but within the other one.

Growing up in that little town in the heart of the dust bowl, I do not know how I could have survived without the words of the printed page, of books. I wish that I could rhapsodize about the natural beauties of the place, the rich and varied landscape, but I cannot. It was rather bleak, surrounded by wheat and maize fields, with few trees. I recall being out on oil rigs on various jobs, looking out across the barren country treeless from horizon to horizon, listening to the chains beating against the derrick in the ceaseless wind, and waiting, waiting for life to come to some kind of point. But it only seemed to come to a point on the printed page, and so I lived, when I could, among books, and words filled up the empty horizon and made for me a necessary world.

Later, as a young man I happened to be sitting alone in a movie theater waiting for the darkness, like sleep, to descend, and I noticed several rows in front a woman speaking to someone hidden in the seat beside her. The someone was apparently her child, for she doted on it, smiling expressively, occasionally laughing, talking to it, reaching over to smooth its dress or collar. She even went to the concession stand and brought back a box of popcorn for it. After the movie started, this constant yet unobtrusive stream of maternal affection continued, and when the movie ended, I waited to see what the child looked like. The mother rose and walked out with her hand outstretched as if the child hidden behind the row of seats were following at arm's length, but when they reached the aisle, the mother's hand was holding nothing at all. There was no child. And the woman walked up the aisle and out of the theater with her hand held out to nothing, occasionally looking down and speaking to the child she only imagined.

To this day I cannot quite explain why that scene will not leave me. Surely there are terror and mystery in it, and perhaps, ignorant of and untouched by the human experience behind the scene, I can afford to be fascinated by it. Perhaps the woman and her imagined child represent for me the unspeakable outer limits of human tragedy, or some arctic zone of the imagination where reality is no longer surpassed but cruelly and impossibly replaced. I think, though, that it is the fact of absence in the scene that will not let me forget it: the absence beneath the mother's hand as she walked out of the theater, the absence of apparent meaning, the absence of a real rather than an imagined life, absences like so many lighted windows as you walk through a strange city, wanting to fill them with imaginary lives and words and stories.

And so, driving past the abandoned basketball court or the small, slowly dying farmtown in Kansas, or sitting before the blank screen after the audience has filed out, I am worried—inspired is certainly not the right word—into the interesting struggle called writing: slow, halting gestures toward that centripetal universe at whose center I stood as a boy on Kansas Avenue. I think now of that struggle as it occurred many years later about four o'clock in the morning in a darkened room, darkened because my two-year-old son was sleeping fitfully nearby. There was some trouble in my life, and it seemed to be echoed in the growls of a pack of dogs that passed beneath the window regularly at that time as they roamed the neighborhood overturning trash cans in search of scraps. I was trying to write a poem about my father, a poem I had struggled to write many times before about lathework and the machine shop and the peculiar beauty of blue steel shavings under lamplight. But then, as now, it had no ending, no place to go. And then the dogs moved on and there was only the silence, and I found myself writing, *let words be steel, let them make fine, thin lines across an empty page.* It was a beginning, I thought, I am almost home. I could hear my son's easy breathing in the next room, the slow grind of the lathe, the sigh of the shavings as they dropped into the oil and water below.